HANOI VIETNAM
TRAVEL GUIDE
2025

Discover the Timeless Charm
and Vibrant Culture of
Vietnam's Capital

CLARA WRIGHT

TABLE OF CONTENTS

1.0 Introduction to Hanoi: The Heart of Vietnam

Hanoi, the capital of Vietnam, is a city where tradition and modernity coexist harmoniously, offering visitors a rich tapestry of history, culture, and vibrant energy. As one of the oldest capitals in the world, Hanoi is not only the political and cultural hub of the nation but also an increasingly popular destination for travelers seeking an authentic Vietnamese experience. From its ancient temples and pagodas to its bustling streets, Hanoi invites exploration with its unique blend of old-world charm and contemporary vibrancy.

Overview of Hanoi: A City of History, Culture, and Tradition

Hanoi's distinctiveness lies in its fusion of history and culture. The city is a living museum, where ancient architecture and traditions are woven into the fabric of daily life. With its winding streets, historical landmarks, and vibrant markets, Hanoi presents a beautiful contrast between its colonial past and rapidly developing modernity. The Old Quarter, with its narrow streets and traditional shophouses, is a prime example of this juxtaposition, offering visitors a glimpse of what Hanoi might have looked like centuries ago. At the same time, the city is home to contemporary art galleries, stylish cafes, and high-end shopping districts, showcasing its evolving cultural landscape.

A Brief History of Hanoi: From Ancient Times to Modern Vibrancy

Hanoi's history spans over a thousand years, with its origins tracing back to the 3rd century BCE when it was known as Thang Long. The city became the political capital of Vietnam during the Ly Dynasty in 1010 and has remained the center of Vietnamese culture ever since. Over the centuries, Hanoi has been influenced by various dynasties, foreign invaders, and colonial powers, each leaving its mark on the city's architecture, cuisine, and traditions.

The French colonization of Vietnam in the 19th century brought with it an architectural and cultural shift, with colonial buildings and wide boulevards still visible in modern Hanoi today. After Vietnam's reunification in 1975, the city underwent rapid growth, evolving into a bustling metropolis that is both a preserve of history and a modern urban center. Today, Hanoi is a dynamic city that embraces its past while looking toward the future, making it an exciting destination for travelers.

Why Visit Hanoi in 2025: Key Highlights and Attractions

Hanoi in 2025 promises to be an even more attractive destination for tourists, offering an abundance of cultural, historical, and natural experiences. Key highlights include:

The Old Quarter: The historical heart of Hanoi, where ancient streets are named after the goods once traded there. Here, visitors can explore narrow alleys, admire the architecture, and sample the city's renowned street food.

Hoan Kiem Lake: A serene oasis in the center of the city, where visitors can enjoy peaceful walks or take in the view of the Ngoc Son Temple perched on an island.

The Temple of Literature: A Confucian temple and Vietnam's first university, offering insight into the country's intellectual history.

The Hanoi Opera House: An elegant example of French colonial architecture, hosting world-class performances.

The Museum of Ethnology: A fascinating museum that showcases Vietnam's diverse ethnic groups through exhibits and artifacts.

These attractions, along with a burgeoning food scene, contemporary art galleries, and a growing number of international events, make Hanoi a must-visit destination in 2025.

The Unique Charm of Hanoi: From Old-World Charm to Contemporary Energy

What sets Hanoi apart is its ability to maintain a sense of its ancient traditions while embracing modernity. The city's Old Quarter, with its labyrinthine streets and centuries-old architecture, exudes an atmosphere of nostalgia. In contrast, the newer districts of Hanoi are teeming with energy, with sleek skyscrapers, trendy cafes, and lively markets. This duality gives Hanoi a distinct personality, where visitors can immerse themselves in the past during a visit to the ancient temples or take in the modernity of its cafes and restaurants.

This mix of old-world charm and contemporary energy is reflected in the city's people—warm, welcoming, and eager to share their culture with visitors. Hanoi's markets, where vendors sell everything from fresh produce to intricate handicrafts, are a microcosm of the city's vibrancy and diversity.

What to Expect: Culture, Climate, and Experiences in Hanoi

Hanoi offers a range of cultural experiences, from exploring its historical landmarks to engaging with local traditions and customs. Visitors can sample Hanoi's famous street food, such as pho (noodle soup), bun cha (grilled pork with noodles), and egg coffee, at bustling street-side eateries or upscale restaurants.

Hanoi's climate is characterized by four distinct seasons: spring, summer, autumn, and winter. The best time to visit is from October to April, when the weather is cooler and more pleasant, especially for outdoor activities like sightseeing. Summers can be hot and humid, with temperatures reaching up to 35°C (95°F), but the city's lively atmosphere and air-conditioned cafes provide a respite.

The experiences in Hanoi are not limited to sightseeing. Visitors can also explore the city's vibrant arts scene, attend local festivals, or take a day trip to nearby attractions like Halong Bay or the Ninh Binh region, known for its stunning karst landscapes.

In conclusion, Hanoi is a city that offers a unique blend of history, culture, and modernity. Whether you're exploring ancient temples, wandering the charming streets of the Old Quarter, or enjoying contemporary cuisine in a hip café, Hanoi presents an authentic and immersive experience that is sure to captivate any traveler. As the city continues to evolve, it remains a destination that should not be missed in 2025.

2.0 How to Get to Hanoi

Hanoi, the vibrant capital of Vietnam, is easily accessible by air, land, and public transportation. Whether you're flying in from abroad, traveling overland, or navigating the city once you arrive, Hanoi offers multiple options to reach and explore its rich culture and history. Here's a comprehensive guide to getting to Hanoi, as well as essential travel tips.

Getting to Hanoi by Air: Noi Bai International Airport and Regional Flights

The primary entry point for international travelers is Noi Bai International Airport (HAN), located approximately 30 kilometers (18 miles) north of Hanoi's city center. This bustling airport serves as a hub for both domestic and international flights, connecting the city to major global destinations. Vietnam Airlines, VietJet Air, and Bamboo Airways are some of the key carriers offering direct flights to Hanoi from cities across Asia, Europe, and the Middle East. Frequent connections are available from cities like Bangkok, Singapore, Hong Kong, and Doha.

For regional travel, many flights operate from other Vietnamese cities like Ho Chi Minh City and Da Nang. Budget carriers such as VietJet and Jetstar Pacific make it convenient for travelers already in Vietnam or Southeast Asia to reach Hanoi affordably. From the airport, visitors can take taxis, airport shuttles, or ride-hailing services like Grab to get into the city. There is also an option to take a public bus, which is a more budget-friendly method of transportation.

Overland Travel: Buses and Trains from Neighboring Cities and Countries

Hanoi is well-connected to other parts of Vietnam and neighboring countries through bus and train routes. Overland travel can be an excellent option for those already in the region.

Buses: Buses are a common and affordable way to travel to Hanoi from nearby cities. Mai Linh and The Sinh Tourist are popular bus operators that provide services between Hanoi and cities like Ho Chi Minh City, Da Nang, and Hue. These journeys can take anywhere from 12 to 24 hours, depending on the distance, but buses are relatively inexpensive and offer both sleeper and regular seating.

Trains: Vietnam's extensive rail network offers another scenic way to travel to Hanoi. The Reunification Express is the most popular train route, running from Ho Chi Minh City to Hanoi. The journey can take between 12 to 24 hours, depending on the route. Train travel is comfortable and allows you to enjoy beautiful countryside views. Hanoi's Railway Station is centrally located, making it easy to reach hotels and attractions from the station.

International Bus and Train Services: If you're traveling from neighboring countries like China or Laos, there are international bus and train services available. For example, buses from Vientiane (Laos) and Kunming (China) connect directly to Hanoi. Though these journeys are long, they offer a chance to see the countryside and are an affordable alternative for international travelers.

Public Transportation in Hanoi: Taxis, Ride-Hailing Apps, and Bicycles

Once you've arrived in Hanoi, navigating the city is easy with multiple local transportation options:

Taxis: Taxis are a common mode of transport and can be hailed on the street or booked by phone. Popular taxi companies in Hanoi include Mai Linh and Vinasun. Taxis are metered, and the fares are relatively affordable by international standards.

Ride-Hailing Apps: Services like Grab and Gojek have become the most convenient and widely used means of getting around Hanoi. With a smartphone, you can easily book a car or motorbike, with transparent pricing and the option to pay via the app. Grab is particularly useful in Hanoi, where traffic can be dense.

Bicycles: Hanoi is known for being a bicycle-friendly city, especially in areas like the Old Quarter and around Hoan Kiem Lake. Many hotels and hostels offer free or rental bicycles to their guests. Exploring by bicycle is a relaxing and eco-friendly way to discover the city's many charming streets and hidden gems.

The Best Times to Visit Hanoi: Weather, Festivals, and Seasonal Highlights

Hanoi experiences four distinct seasons, making the best time to visit highly dependent on personal preferences.

Spring (March to April): Spring in Hanoi is one of the most pleasant times to visit, with mild temperatures, clear skies, and blossoming flowers.

The city is vibrant, and this period is perfect for outdoor activities and sightseeing.

Summer (May to August): Summer can be hot and humid, with temperatures soaring above 35°C (95°F). This is also the rainy season, so expect occasional downpours. However, fewer tourists visit during these months, which means you can enjoy the attractions without the crowds.

Autumn (September to November): Autumn is arguably the best time to visit Hanoi. The weather is cool and dry, with temperatures ranging from 20°C to 25°C (68°F to 77°F), making it perfect for walking around the city. This period also coincides with the Mid-Autumn Festival, a significant cultural event featuring lantern festivals and mooncakes.

Winter (December to February): Winter is cooler, and temperatures can dip to around 10°C (50°F). While the weather is dry, the cooler air may not be ideal for those who prefer warmth. However, this is the off-season, and you'll encounter fewer tourists, allowing you to experience Hanoi more authentically.

Visa and Entry Requirements: Essential Travel Information for Foreign Visitors

Vietnam has specific visa and entry requirements for foreign travelers. Nationals of certain countries, such as Japan, South Korea, and several European nations, can enter Vietnam without a visa for stays of up to 15 days. For longer stays, visitors must apply for a tourist visa.

The easiest way to obtain a visa is through the e-Visa system, which allows travelers from eligible countries to apply online before their trip. Alternatively, travelers can apply for a visa through a Vietnamese embassy or consulate in their home country. Ensure that your passport is valid for at least six months beyond your planned arrival date in Vietnam.

In conclusion, getting to Hanoi is easy with multiple options for air, bus, and train travel. Once you arrive, navigating the city is simple with taxis, ride-hailing apps, and bicycle rentals. To ensure a smooth visit, check the weather and festival calendar to find the best time for your trip, and be sure to confirm your visa requirements before traveling.

3.0 Exploring Hanoi's Old Quarter

Hanoi's Old Quarter is the beating heart of the city, where history, culture, and daily life intersect in a vibrant display of narrow streets, traditional architecture, and rich local customs. This bustling area is an essential part of any trip to Hanoi, offering a glimpse into the past while embracing the dynamic energy of modern life. Here's an in-depth look at what to explore in Hanoi's Old Quarter.

The Old Quarter: Hanoi's Historic Heart and Cultural Hub

The Old Quarter, or Hanoi's 36 Streets, is one of the city's most fascinating neighborhoods, where every corner is steeped in history. This area dates back to the 13th century, and its name comes from the 36 streets, each once dedicated to a specific trade or craft. Walking through the Old Quarter is like stepping into a living museum, where old traditions blend seamlessly with the present. The quarter retains its old-world charm, with traditional Hanoi architecture, colonial-era buildings, and ancient temples tucked away among the busy streets.

The Old Quarter is not just a tourist attraction; it is a thriving center of daily life for Hanoi's residents. Local markets, street vendors, and small businesses fill the narrow lanes, and the area exudes an atmosphere of constant hustle and bustle. Visitors can experience the cultural richness of Hanoi, where both old and new coexist in harmony.

Must-Visit Streets: Exploring the 36 Streets and Their Unique Traditions

The 36 Streets are the backbone of the Old Quarter, each street historically known for a specific trade or service. Some of the most famous include:

Hang Bac (Silver Street) – Known for its silversmiths and jewelry shops.

Hang Gai (Silk Street) – Famous for high-quality silks and fabrics, offering beautiful traditional Vietnamese clothing.

Hang Duong (Candy Street) – A sweet tooth's paradise, lined with shops selling traditional Vietnamese sweets and treats.

Hang Cho (Market Street) – Home to local markets offering a variety of goods, from fresh produce to household items.

Exploring these streets is like taking a walk through time, as each one tells a story of Hanoi's historical trades and customs. These vibrant lanes are ideal for wandering, where you can browse through local goods, take in the bustling street scenes, and interact with the friendly vendors.

Top Attractions in the Old Quarter: Hoan Kiem Lake, Ngoc Son Temple, and St. Joseph's Cathedral

While the Old Quarter itself is a treasure trove of experiences, it also houses some of Hanoi's most iconic attractions:

Hoan Kiem Lake: The centerpiece of the Old Quarter, Hoan Kiem Lake is a serene and picturesque spot. The lake is wrapped in local legends, most notably the myth of the Legend of the Sword, where a giant turtle is said to have surfaced after a sword was returned to the gods. The Turtle Tower, situated in the middle of the lake, is a popular photo spot. The lake is a hub of activity with locals practicing Tai Chi, walking, or enjoying leisurely boat rides.

Ngoc Son Temple: Situated on an island on Hoan Kiem Lake, the Ngoc Son Temple is a must-see for visitors. The temple, dedicated to the ancient Vietnamese hero General Tran Hung Dao, is connected to the shore by the iconic Red Bridge (Thap Rua). It's an important historical and cultural site that offers a peaceful respite from the busy streets of the Old Quarter.

St. Joseph's Cathedral: Built in the late 19th century, this Gothic-style cathedral is one of Hanoi's oldest churches. Its stunning architecture and tall spires make it a striking feature in the Old Quarter, and its atmosphere is peaceful and serene, providing a quiet break from the city's vibrant energy.

Shopping in the Old Quarter: Souvenirs, Local Markets, and Street Vendors

The Old Quarter is a shopper's paradise, offering everything from high-end handicrafts to quirky souvenirs. Some of the best places to shop include:

Local Markets: The Old Quarter is home to many vibrant local markets, such as Dong Xuan Market, where visitors can buy everything from clothing to handicrafts and fresh produce. The market is the heart of the local trading scene, and wandering through its aisles offers a glimpse into daily life in Hanoi.

Street Vendors: The streets of the Old Quarter are lined with street vendors offering handmade goods, clothing, trinkets, and art. These markets are ideal for picking up unique souvenirs, such as lacquerware, silk scarves, and traditional Vietnamese ceramics.

Boutiques and Art Galleries: In addition to street vendors, the Old Quarter is also home to small boutique shops and art galleries where visitors can purchase contemporary Vietnamese art, antiques, and custom-made items. These shops offer a more personalized shopping experience.

Dining in the Old Quarter: Street Food, Pho, and Traditional Vietnamese Dishes

No visit to Hanoi's Old Quarter would be complete without indulging in the city's legendary food scene. The area is famous for its street food, where visitors can sample traditional Vietnamese dishes at roadside stalls or local eateries. Here are some must-try dishes:

Pho: Hanoi is the birthplace of Pho, Vietnam's most famous dish. The Old Quarter is filled with Pho stalls, each offering its own variation of this savory soup made with rice noodles, beef (or chicken), and fragrant herbs. Pho Gia Truyen is one of the most famous spots to enjoy this dish.

Banh Mi: A Vietnamese sandwich made with a crispy baguette, Banh Mi is a perfect street food snack. It's typically filled with meats, pickled vegetables, and herbs, and it's a great way to experience the fusion of French and Vietnamese culinary influences.

Bun Cha: A Hanoi specialty, Bun Cha consists of grilled pork served with vermicelli noodles, fresh herbs, and dipping sauce. It's a beloved local dish, and several eateries in the Old Quarter specialize in this flavorful dish.

Egg Coffee: For something sweet, try Egg Coffee (Cà Phê Trứng), a Hanoi original. This creamy, frothy coffee is made with egg yolk, sugar, condensed milk, and robust Vietnamese coffee, creating a decadent treat.

Exploring the Old Quarter is a sensory experience, offering a blend of history, culture, shopping, and delicious food. Whether you're strolling through its vibrant streets, soaking in its top attractions, or sampling its famous street food, the Old Quarter is a place where the past and present come alive in the heart of Hanoi.

4.0 Must-See Attractions in Hanoi

Hanoi, the vibrant capital of Vietnam, is a city brimming with history, culture, and a fascinating blend of ancient traditions and colonial influences. Whether you're a history buff, an art lover, or simply curious about the local culture, Hanoi offers a wide array of attractions that will leave you with lasting memories. Here are some of the must-see attractions in this dynamic city.

The Temple of Literature: Vietnam's Oldest University and Cultural Landmark

The Temple of Literature (Văn Miếu), established in 1070 during the reign of the Ly Dynasty, is one of Hanoi's most iconic cultural landmarks. Originally built to honor Confucius, this site served as

Vietnam's first national university, educating scholars and officials for nearly 800 years. Today, the temple is a serene space for reflection and a key symbol of Vietnam's long history of education and intellectual achievement.

Visitors can stroll through its five courtyards, each representing different stages of education and enlightenment. The tranquil surroundings, combined with the intricate architecture and historical significance, make the Temple of Literature a must-visit spot. Don't miss the Stelae of Doctors, which are stone tablets inscribed with the names of successful students, and the Great Middle Hall, where offerings are made to Confucius. The temple's well-preserved beauty and rich cultural history make it an essential stop for anyone visiting Hanoi.

Ho Chi Minh Mausoleum: The Final Resting Place of Vietnam's Founding Father

No visit to Hanoi is complete without a visit to the Ho Chi Minh Mausoleum (Lăng Chủ Tịch Hồ Chí Minh), the final resting place of President Ho Chi Minh, the revolutionary leader who led Vietnam to independence. The mausoleum, a monumental structure, is located in Ba Dinh Square, where Ho Chi Minh declared the country's independence from France in 1945.

The mausoleum itself is an imposing structure made of grey granite, and it stands as a testament to the reverence and respect Ho Chi Minh commands in Vietnam. Visitors can pay their respects to the beloved leader by entering the mausoleum, where his embalmed body is displayed in a glass case, surrounded by an atmosphere of solemnity. The site is part of a larger complex that includes Ho Chi Minh's stilt house and the Presidential Palace, where you can learn more about his life and legacy.

The Hanoi Opera House: French Colonial Architecture and Cultural Performances

Built in 1911 during French colonial rule, the Hanoi Opera House (Nhà Hát Lớn Hà Nội) is a stunning example of French colonial architecture. Inspired by the Palais Garnier in Paris, the opera house features an ornate facade, classical columns, and elegant interiors, making it one of the most beautiful buildings in Hanoi.

The opera house is not only a visual marvel but also a cultural hub that hosts various performances, from classical music and opera to traditional Vietnamese dance and theater. Whether you're attending a performance or simply admiring its architecture, the Hanoi Opera House offers a glimpse into the cultural richness of the city and the legacy of French influence on Hanoi's urban landscape.

The Hanoi Hilton (Hoa Lo Prison): A Historical Insight into Vietnam's Past

The Hoa Lo Prison, also known as the Hanoi Hilton, is a stark reminder of the country's turbulent history during the colonial period and the Vietnam War. Built by the French in the late 19th century to imprison Vietnamese political dissidents, the prison was later used by North Vietnam to hold American POWs during the war. Today, the prison has been partially preserved as a museum, offering visitors a sobering look at the hardships faced by prisoners and the resilience of the Vietnamese people.

The museum features exhibits on both the French colonial era and the Vietnam War, with displays about the brutal conditions faced by prisoners and their fight for independence. It also provides insight into the stories of American POWs, including John McCain, who was held there during the conflict. The Hoa Lo Prison is a must-see for those interested in learning about Vietnam's struggles for freedom and independence.

The Vietnam Fine Arts Museum: A Showcase of Traditional and Contemporary Art

For art enthusiasts, the Vietnam Fine Arts Museum (Bảo Tàng Mỹ Thuật Việt Nam) is a treasure trove of both traditional and modern Vietnamese art.

Located in a beautifully restored colonial building, the museum houses an extensive collection of paintings, sculptures, and ceramics that trace the evolution of Vietnamese art from ancient times to the present.

The museum's collection includes works from the Dai Viet period, showcasing ancient sculptures and ceramics, as well as more recent works from the French colonial era and the modern art scene. One of the highlights is the display of Vietnamese folk art, including traditional lacquer paintings, watercolor pieces, and stone carvings. The museum is an excellent place to gain insight into the cultural evolution of Vietnam through its artistic expressions.

Conclusion

Hanoi is a city that offers a rich tapestry of historical, cultural, and architectural landmarks. From the intellectual legacy of the Temple of Literature to the solemnity of the Ho Chi Minh Mausoleum, and the grandeur of the Hanoi Opera House, each attraction reveals a different facet of this vibrant city. The Hoa Lo Prison and the Vietnam Fine Arts Museum provide deeper insight into Vietnam's tumultuous past and the resilience of its people. A visit to these must-see attractions offers a deeper understanding of Hanoi's unique character and its significance in Vietnam's history.

5.0 Must-See Attractions in Hanoi

Hanoi, the vibrant capital of Vietnam, is a city brimming with history, culture, and a fascinating blend of ancient traditions and colonial influences. Whether you're a history buff, an art lover, or simply curious about the local culture, Hanoi offers a wide array of attractions that will leave you with lasting memories. Here are some of the must-see attractions in this dynamic city.

The Temple of Literature: Vietnam's Oldest University and Cultural Landmark

The Temple of Literature (Văn Miếu), established in 1070 during the reign of the Ly Dynasty, is one of Hanoi's most iconic cultural landmarks. Originally built to honor Confucius, this site served as

Vietnam's first national university, educating scholars and officials for nearly 800 years. Today, the temple is a serene space for reflection and a key symbol of Vietnam's long history of education and intellectual achievement.

Visitors can stroll through its five courtyards, each representing different stages of education and enlightenment. The tranquil surroundings, combined with the intricate architecture and historical significance, make the Temple of Literature a must-visit spot. Don't miss the Stelae of Doctors, which are stone tablets inscribed with the names of successful students, and the Great Middle Hall, where offerings are made to Confucius. The temple's well-preserved beauty and rich cultural history make it an essential stop for anyone visiting Hanoi.

Ho Chi Minh Mausoleum: The Final Resting Place of Vietnam's Founding Father

No visit to Hanoi is complete without a visit to the Ho Chi Minh Mausoleum (Lăng Chủ Tịch Hồ Chí Minh), the final resting place of President Ho Chi Minh, the revolutionary leader who led Vietnam to independence. The mausoleum, a monumental structure, is located in Ba Dinh Square, where Ho Chi Minh declared the country's independence from France in 1945.

The mausoleum itself is an imposing structure made of grey granite, and it stands as a testament to the reverence and respect Ho Chi Minh commands in Vietnam. Visitors can pay their respects to the beloved leader by entering the mausoleum, where his embalmed body is displayed in a glass case, surrounded by an atmosphere of solemnity. The site is part of a larger complex that includes Ho Chi Minh's stilt house and the Presidential Palace, where you can learn more about his life and legacy.

The Hanoi Opera House: French Colonial Architecture and Cultural Performances

Built in 1911 during French colonial rule, the Hanoi Opera House (Nhà Hát Lớn Hà Nội) is a stunning example of French colonial architecture. Inspired by the Palais Garnier in Paris, the opera house features an ornate facade, classical columns, and elegant interiors, making it one of the most beautiful buildings in Hanoi.

The opera house is not only a visual marvel but also a cultural hub that hosts various performances, from classical music and opera to traditional Vietnamese dance and theater. Whether you're attending a performance or simply admiring its architecture, the Hanoi Opera House offers a glimpse into the cultural richness of the city and the legacy of French influence on Hanoi's urban landscape.

The Hanoi Hilton (Hoa Lo Prison): A Historical Insight into Vietnam's Past

The Hoa Lo Prison, also known as the Hanoi Hilton, is a stark reminder of the country's turbulent history during the colonial period and the Vietnam War. Built by the French in the late 19th century to imprison Vietnamese political dissidents, the prison was later used by North Vietnam to hold American POWs during the war. Today, the prison has been partially preserved as a museum, offering visitors a sobering look at the hardships faced by prisoners and the resilience of the Vietnamese people.

The museum features exhibits on both the French colonial era and the Vietnam War, with displays about the brutal conditions faced by prisoners and their fight for independence. It also provides insight into the stories of American POWs, including John McCain, who was held there during the conflict. The Hoa Lo Prison is a must-see for those interested in learning about Vietnam's struggles for freedom and independence.

The Vietnam Fine Arts Museum: A Showcase of Traditional and Contemporary Art

For art enthusiasts, the Vietnam Fine Arts Museum (Bảo Tàng Mỹ Thuật Việt Nam) is a treasure trove of both traditional and modern Vietnamese art.

Located in a beautifully restored colonial building, the museum houses an extensive collection of paintings, sculptures, and ceramics that trace the evolution of Vietnamese art from ancient times to the present.

The museum's collection includes works from the Dai Viet period, showcasing ancient sculptures and ceramics, as well as more recent works from the French colonial era and the modern art scene. One of the highlights is the display of Vietnamese folk art, including traditional lacquer paintings, watercolor pieces, and stone carvings. The museum is an excellent place to gain insight into the cultural evolution of Vietnam through its artistic expressions.

Conclusion

Hanoi is a city that offers a rich tapestry of historical, cultural, and architectural landmarks. From the intellectual legacy of the Temple of Literature to the solemnity of the Ho Chi Minh Mausoleum, and the grandeur of the Hanoi Opera House, each attraction reveals a different facet of this vibrant city. The Hoa Lo Prison and the Vietnam Fine Arts Museum provide deeper insight into Vietnam's tumultuous past and the resilience of its people. A visit to these must-see attractions offers a deeper understanding of Hanoi's unique character and its significance in Vietnam's history.

6.0 Outdoor Activities and Parks in Hanoi

Hanoi, with its vibrant streets and historic landmarks, is also home to some remarkable outdoor spaces that offer a refreshing break from the hustle and bustle of the city. Whether you're looking for a peaceful lake to relax by, a scenic park to explore, or an adventure in nature, Hanoi has a variety of outdoor activities and parks to enjoy.

Hoan Kiem Lake: A Relaxing Escape in the City Center

Hoan Kiem Lake (Lake of the Returned Sword) is one of Hanoi's most iconic landmarks, located right in the heart of the city. The serene lake is a popular spot for both locals and visitors seeking a peaceful retreat amidst the urban chaos. Legend has it that the lake was named after a magical sword that was returned by a giant turtle to its rightful owner, a historical tale that adds a mystical charm to the setting.

A walk around the lake, especially in the early morning, offers a tranquil escape with beautiful views of the surrounding trees, the Ngoc Son Temple situated on a small island in the lake, and the Red Bridge that connects it to the temple. Locals often practice Tai Chi or jog along the pathways, creating a calm and peaceful atmosphere. It's a perfect spot for leisurely strolls, photography, or simply relaxing by the water.

West Lake (Ho Tay): Boating, Walking, and Scenic Views

West Lake (Ho Tay), Hanoi's largest lake, offers a larger expanse of water and a more relaxed, scenic environment compared to Hoan Kiem Lake. Located to the northwest of the Old Quarter, West Lake is known for its stunning sunsets, peaceful walks, and a variety of outdoor activities. It's a popular spot for locals to take leisurely walks or cycle around its perimeter.

Visitors can enjoy boating on the lake, offering a unique perspective of the surrounding landscape and an opportunity to unwind on the water. The area is also dotted with beautiful gardens, temples, and historic sites, such as the Tran Quoc Pagoda, one of the oldest Buddhist temples in Vietnam. Numerous cafes and restaurants line the lake, offering perfect spots to relax while enjoying the view. West Lake is also home to cherry blossoms in the spring, adding an extra layer of beauty to the landscape.

Hanoi Botanical Garden: Exploring Green Spaces and Natural Beauty

For nature lovers, the Hanoi Botanical Garden (Vườn Bách Thảo) provides a serene and expansive green space to explore. Located near the Ho Chi Minh Mausoleum, this garden offers lush greenery, a variety of tropical plants, and peaceful walking paths that wind through the trees. The garden is home to a large collection of indigenous and exotic plant species, making it a great place for plant enthusiasts to admire the variety of flora.

The botanical garden is not just a place for plants; it's also an ideal spot for a relaxing picnic, family outings, or simply enjoying nature in the city. The spaciousness and tranquility of the garden provide a refreshing contrast to the urban noise, making it an excellent retreat for visitors looking to reconnect with nature.

Ba Vi National Park: Hiking, Nature Trails, and Scenic Views

For a more adventurous outdoor experience, a trip to Ba Vi National Park is highly recommended. Located about 60 kilometers west of Hanoi, Ba Vi offers a breathtaking natural landscape with mountainous terrain, lush forests, and scenic views of the surrounding countryside. The park is known for its hiking trails, ranging from easy walks to more challenging mountain treks.

The summit of Ba Vi Mountain offers panoramic views of the surrounding valleys and forests, while the park is home to diverse wildlife, including various species of birds and butterflies. The park also boasts historic sites, including the Ba Vi Temple and the Cao Son Pagoda, which add cultural interest to the natural beauty of the area.

Ba Vi National Park is an ideal destination for those seeking a blend of adventure, nature, and history, making it perfect for hiking, photography, and nature walks.

Cycling Tours: Discovering Hanoi's Green Spaces and Surroundings by Bike

Cycling is one of the best ways to explore Hanoi's green spaces and the surrounding countryside. Several companies offer cycling tours that take visitors through picturesque neighborhoods, tranquil lakes, and lush countryside. These tours are ideal for those looking to get off the beaten path and explore the city's quieter, more scenic areas at a relaxed pace.

The tours often include routes around West Lake, through Hanoi's green parks, and along the Red River. For those interested in exploring beyond the city limits, longer cycling trips can take you to rural villages and farmland just outside Hanoi, offering a unique perspective of traditional Vietnamese life. Cycling provides a more intimate experience of Hanoi's natural beauty, giving visitors the chance to see the city and its surroundings from a fresh perspective.

Conclusion

Hanoi's outdoor activities and parks provide a refreshing escape from the city's fast pace, offering everything from serene lakes and green spaces to nature trails and mountain hikes. Whether you're seeking relaxation in Hoan Kiem Lake, an active day at Ba Vi National Park, or a leisurely cycling tour through the city's scenic areas, Hanoi's outdoor attractions are sure to captivate nature lovers and adventure seekers alike. These parks and green spaces offer a perfect blend of tranquility, natural beauty, and opportunities for outdoor exploration, making them essential to any visit to the Vietnamese capital.

7.0 Day Trips and Nearby Destinations from Hanoi

Hanoi's central location makes it an excellent base for exploring some of Vietnam's most scenic and culturally rich destinations. Whether you're drawn to stunning natural landscapes, historic sites, or immersive cultural experiences, there are a number of day trips and nearby destinations that showcase the diversity of Northern Vietnam. Below are some of the top excursions you can enjoy from Hanoi.

Halong Bay: UNESCO World Heritage Site and Natural Wonder

Just a 2.5-hour drive from Hanoi, Halong Bay is one of Vietnam's most iconic natural wonders, known for its limestone karsts and emerald-green waters. A UNESCO World Heritage Site, Halong Bay is dotted with over 1,600 islands and islets, creating a stunning seascape that attracts travelers from around the world.

A day trip to Halong Bay typically involves a boat cruise that lets you explore its famous islands, caves, and fishing villages. Sung Sot Cave (Surprise Cave) and Ti Top Island are among the most popular attractions, offering awe-inspiring views of the bay from higher viewpoints. Visitors can also enjoy activities like kayaking, swimming, or simply relaxing on the boat while marveling at the dramatic rock formations. Whether you choose to take a short day tour or a longer overnight cruise, Halong Bay provides an unforgettable experience in nature.

Ninh Binh: Limestone Karsts, Tam Coc, and Hoa Lu Ancient Capital

Ninh Binh, often referred to as "Halong Bay on land," is just a 2-hour drive from Hanoi. This province is renowned for its striking limestone karsts, lush valleys, and picturesque rivers. The Tam Coc area is famous for its boat rides along the Ngo Dong River, where you'll glide through caves and past towering cliffs that rise dramatically from the water, offering a serene and scenic experience.

For history enthusiasts, Ninh Binh also offers the ancient capital of Hoa Lu, a historic site that was once the center of Vietnamese political power during the 10th and 11th centuries. The ancient temples and pagodas here honor kings who ruled during this period. Additionally, a visit to Bich Dong Pagoda, set against the backdrop of limestone mountains, provides a peaceful retreat. Ninh Binh is perfect for those looking to combine natural beauty with a touch of Vietnam's ancient history.

Perfume Pagoda: A Spiritual Journey in the Countryside

Located about 60 kilometers southwest of Hanoi, the Perfume Pagoda (Chùa Hương) is one of the most important religious sites in Vietnam. The journey to the pagoda is as much a part of the experience as the destination itself. Visitors take a boat ride along the ** Yen Stream**, passing through lush countryside and picturesque limestone mountains. The boat ride is followed by a hike up to the main Perfume Pagoda complex, which includes temples, pagodas, and caves nestled in the hills.

Perfume Pagoda is a site of pilgrimage for Buddhists, particularly during the Lunar New Year, when thousands of visitors come to pay respects and seek blessings. The atmosphere is peaceful, making it an ideal spot for those interested in spirituality, nature, and Vietnamese cultural traditions. The surrounding area is filled with stunning views and the sound of chanting monks, providing an unforgettable day trip from Hanoi.

Mai Chau: A Rural Escape for Nature and Cultural Experiences

If you're looking to experience the rural charm of Northern Vietnam, Mai Chau is an excellent destination. Located about 3 to 4 hours from Hanoi, Mai Chau is a tranquil valley surrounded by rice paddies, ethnic minority villages, and stunning mountain scenery. The area is predominantly inhabited by the White Thai ethnic group, and visitors can enjoy a cultural immersion by staying in traditional stilt houses, learning about local customs, and sampling regional cuisine.

Mai Chau offers a variety of outdoor activities, such as cycling through the valley, trekking to nearby villages, or simply relaxing and enjoying the breathtaking natural surroundings. The area is known for its fresh air, peaceful atmosphere, and unique cultural traditions, making it a perfect escape from the urban bustle of Hanoi.

Duong Lam Village: An Ancient Vietnamese Village and Historic Site

For a glimpse into traditional Vietnamese life, a visit to Duong Lam Village, located about 50 kilometers from Hanoi, offers a fascinating journey into the country's rural past. This ancient village is home to well-preserved 150-year-old houses, some of which are made from laterite stone, a material that's increasingly rare in Vietnam today. The village's architecture and landscapes have remained largely unchanged for centuries, providing a rare look into Vietnam's traditional rural life.

Highlights of a visit to Duong Lam include exploring the village's historical temples, such as the Mong Phu Temple, dedicated to the village's founders. You can also visit the Mia Pagoda, which houses several statues of Buddhist deities. The peaceful atmosphere, ancient houses, and rural surroundings make Duong Lam Village a wonderful place to experience Vietnamese history and culture firsthand.

Conclusion

Hanoi is the perfect starting point for a variety of day trips that offer unique experiences of Vietnam's natural beauty, rich history, and cultural diversity. From the stunning limestone landscapes of Halong Bay and Ninh Binh, to the spiritual journey to

Perfume Pagoda and the rural escapes to Mai Chau and Duong Lam Village, there is no shortage of remarkable destinations near Hanoi. Whether you're interested in outdoor adventures, historical exploration, or cultural immersion, these day trips provide a well-rounded experience of Northern Vietnam that will make your visit even more memorable.

8.0 Food and Drink in Hanoi

Hanoi, the capital of Vietnam, offers a vibrant culinary scene that is both rich in history and diverse in flavors. Known for its delicious street food, fresh ingredients, and unique dishes, the city provides an unforgettable food experience for every traveler. Whether you're sampling local specialties or enjoying a refined dining experience, Hanoi's food culture is sure to delight.

Vietnamese Cuisine: An Introduction to Hanoi's Local Specialties

Hanoi's cuisine is a blend of sweet, sour, salty, and spicy flavors, often balanced in harmony. Central to Hanoi's culinary identity is the use of fresh herbs, rice, noodles, and seafood. The food is typically light, with an emphasis on fresh vegetables, local meats, and aromatic broths. A hallmark of Hanoi's cuisine is Pho, the famous Vietnamese noodle soup, and many of the city's dishes showcase a unique northern twist, differing from the southern and central regions in terms of flavors and ingredients.

Popular northern specialties include Cha Ca (fried fish with turmeric and dill), Bun Thang (a noodle soup with chicken, egg, and pork), and Banh Cuon (steamed rice rolls filled with minced pork and wood ear mushrooms). These dishes highlight Hanoi's tradition of using simple ingredients to create complex, savory flavors.

Street Food in Hanoi: Pho, Bánh Mì, and Bun Cha

When it comes to street food, Hanoi is a haven for food lovers. The city's narrow streets are lined with small stalls serving some of the best-known dishes in Vietnam. Pho, a noodle soup made with either beef (pho bo) or chicken (pho ga), is the quintessential Hanoi dish. The broth, slow-cooked to perfection with aromatic spices like cinnamon, star anise, and ginger, is served with flat rice noodles and a variety of fresh herbs. Eating pho in the morning, often with a hot cup of green tea, is a local tradition.

Another iconic street food is Bánh Mì, a Vietnamese sandwich made with a crispy baguette filled with a variety of meats, pickled vegetables, fresh cilantro, and chili. The perfect fusion of French and Vietnamese culinary traditions, Bánh Mì can be found at food stalls and cafes throughout the city, with endless variations to suit every palate.

For lunch or dinner, try Bun Cha, a delicious dish consisting of grilled pork (usually pork patties and slices of pork belly) served with a sweet-sour dipping sauce and a side of cold rice noodles. It's typically eaten with fresh herbs and fried spring rolls, creating a perfect balance of textures and flavors.

Hanoi's Famous Egg Coffee and Other Unique Beverages

One of the most unique beverages in Hanoi is Egg Coffee (Cà Phê Trứng). Invented in the 1940s, egg coffee is made by whisking egg yolks with sweetened condensed milk, sugar, and vanilla, then adding it to strong Vietnamese coffee. The result is a creamy, velvety drink that has become a must-try for visitors to the city. Served hot or cold, egg coffee is often enjoyed in cozy cafes tucked away in Hanoi's Old Quarter.

In addition to egg coffee, Hanoi offers a range of refreshing beverages. Vietnamese iced coffee (Cà Phê Sữa Đá), made with strong drip coffee and sweetened condensed milk, is a popular choice among locals and visitors alike. For a more exotic taste, try Sinh Tố, a refreshing fruit smoothie made with tropical fruits such as mango, avocado, or papaya.

Dining in Hanoi: Best Restaurants, Cafés, and Fine Dining Experiences

While street food is a key part of Hanoi's food culture, the city also boasts an impressive array of fine dining options. For those looking for a more refined experience, La Verticale is a highly acclaimed restaurant offering French-Vietnamese fusion cuisine. Located in a charming French colonial building, it combines elegant French techniques with local ingredients for a sophisticated dining experience.

For an authentic taste of Vietnamese cuisine in a comfortable setting, Quan An Ngon offers an extensive menu of traditional dishes, from pho to banh xeo (Vietnamese pancakes). The restaurant is renowned for its wide variety of local specialties, prepared by expert chefs using the finest ingredients.

Cafés are also a key part of Hanoi's food scene, with cozy, artsy spots providing the perfect environment for sipping coffee and people-watching. The Hanoi Social Club is a popular café offering a relaxed atmosphere, serving delicious homemade cakes, coffee, and light bites.

Food Markets: Exploring the Culinary Delights at Dong Xuan Market and More

To truly experience the essence of Hanoi's food culture, a visit to the local markets is a must. Dong Xuan Market, the largest and oldest market in Hanoi, is a bustling hub of activity where vendors sell everything from fresh produce to street food. Here, visitors can sample a wide variety of traditional dishes, such as Bánh Cuốn (steamed rice rolls) and Xôi (sticky rice).

For a more immersive experience, explore the Cho Hang Be Market, a smaller, less touristy market known for its fresh fruits, vegetables, and snacks. It's a great place to try some of Hanoi's lesser-known street food, like Bánh Đúc (rice flour cakes) and Chè (Vietnamese sweet soups and desserts).

In addition to these markets, Night Markets in the Old Quarter are perfect for an evening of food exploration, offering everything from grilled meats and seafood to sweet treats and cold drinks.

Conclusion

Hanoi's food scene is a blend of rich history, bold flavors, and a vibrant street culture. From the world-famous Pho to unique local beverages like Egg Coffee, Hanoi offers a food experience unlike any other. Whether indulging in street food, exploring local markets, or dining at upscale restaurants, the city's culinary offerings are sure to leave a lasting impression.

9.0 Shopping in Hanoi

Hanoi, the capital of Vietnam, offers a diverse and vibrant shopping scene, where visitors can discover everything from traditional handicrafts to modern fashion. Whether you're hunting for unique souvenirs, locally-made goods, or luxurious items, Hanoi has something to suit all tastes. The city's markets, streets, and shopping centers provide a rich cultural experience, reflecting the spirit of both ancient traditions and contemporary trends.

Local Markets: Where to Find Unique Vietnamese Handicrafts, Silk, and Souvenirs

Hanoi's local markets are a treasure trove for shoppers looking to bring home authentic Vietnamese handicrafts, silk, and souvenirs. One of the best places to start is Dong Xuan Market, Hanoi's largest and oldest market. Here, you can find an extensive range of items including clothing, textiles, handicrafts, and fresh produce. For those seeking quality Vietnamese silk, silk scarves, and handwoven fabrics, this market is a great place to bargain.

Another notable market is Cho Hang Be, located in the Old Quarter, which specializes in traditional Vietnamese goods, including handcrafted baskets, wooden furniture, and colorful lacquerware. The narrow streets are lined with small shops selling embroidered items, conical hats, and pottery—perfect for those searching for authentic Vietnamese souvenirs.

For a more relaxed shopping experience, visit the Weekend Night Market in Hanoi's Old Quarter. Open every Friday to Sunday, it offers an eclectic mix of handmade jewelry, Vietnamese artwork, and locally made clothing. You'll also find traditional

Vietnamese toys, chopsticks, and wood carvings, making it a great spot to pick up unique gifts for family and friends.

Hanoi's Best Shopping Streets: Trang Tien Plaza, Hang Gai, and the Night Market

Hanoi is home to several bustling shopping streets where visitors can find both high-end brands and locally made goods. Trang Tien Plaza, located near Hoan Kiem Lake, is Hanoi's premier shopping mall. With its sleek, modern architecture, the plaza houses luxury international brands, offering everything from designer clothing and accessories to beauty products and electronics.

For a more traditional shopping experience, Hang Gai Street, also known as Silk Street, is a must-visit. This narrow street is lined with shops specializing in high-quality silk products, including dresses, suits, and scarves. Many stores also sell embroidered linens, wooden carvings, and lacquered furniture, offering a great opportunity to take home beautiful Vietnamese craftsmanship.

The Night Market in the Old Quarter, running through Hang Dao Street, is another great destination for shopping. With hundreds of stalls selling local products, handmade accessories, clothing, and unique souvenirs, the Night Market is a lively hub where both locals and tourists shop into the evening hours.

Traditional Vietnamese Arts and Crafts: Embroidery, Lacquerware, and Pottery

Hanoi is renowned for its traditional arts and crafts, and many shops specialize in these exquisite items. Embroidery, in particular, is one of Vietnam's most celebrated crafts, and you can find beautifully hand-stitched items such as wall hangings, tablecloths, pillowcases, and sheets in shops throughout Hanoi. These pieces are often intricately designed, depicting traditional Vietnamese themes such as landscapes, flowers, and animals.

Lacquerware is another standout product in Hanoi. From plates and bowls to chests and decorative boxes, these high-quality items are crafted using layers of lacquer over wood or bamboo. The process is time-consuming, but the result is stunningly beautiful, with vibrant colors and intricate designs.

Pottery also holds a special place in Vietnamese culture. Hanoi's markets feature handmade ceramic vases, teapots, mugs, and bowls—each piece reflecting the country's artistic heritage. For pottery enthusiasts, Bat Trang Village, located on the outskirts of Hanoi, is a must-visit. The village is famous for its traditional blue-and-white porcelain and ceramics.

Antique Shops and Art Galleries: Unique Finds and Souvenirs

For those seeking unique and rare finds, Hanoi's antique shops and art galleries offer a wealth of treasures. Hang Bac Street, known as Silver Street, is home to several antique shops selling vintage furniture, old coins, antique ceramics, and historical artifacts. Many of these items date back to Vietnam's French colonial period or even earlier.

Hanoi is also home to several art galleries showcasing traditional and contemporary Vietnamese art. The Vietnam Fine Arts Museum is a cultural hub, displaying beautiful paintings, sculptures, and contemporary art. Nearby, galleries in the Old Quarter feature works by local artists, including traditional watercolor paintings, oil paintings, and calligraphy, making them perfect for art lovers in search of a one-of-a-kind souvenir.

Bargaining Tips: How to Shop Like a Local in Hanoi

Bargaining is an essential part of the shopping experience in Hanoi, particularly in the local markets. To shop like a local and get the best prices, it's important to approach the process with patience and a friendly attitude. Here are some useful tips for negotiating:

1. Start with a smile: Building rapport with the vendor will make the bargaining process smoother.

2. Offer a lower price: Vendors typically expect you to negotiate, so it's common to offer around 50% of the asking price, and work your way up from there.

3. Don't be afraid to walk away: If the price is too high, don't hesitate to walk away. Often, the vendor will call you back with a better offer.

4. Pay in cash: Paying with Vietnamese dong in cash (instead of credit cards) can sometimes help you secure a better deal.

By following these tips, you'll not only enjoy a more authentic shopping experience but also gain a deeper understanding of Hanoi's rich culture and traditions.

Conclusion

Hanoi offers an exciting shopping experience, where ancient traditions meet modern trends. From bustling markets to high-end shopping streets and charming antique shops, there's something for everyone. Whether you're looking for intricate lacquerware, handmade silk, or unique antiques, the city's diverse shopping options promise a memorable experience for all.

10.0 Practical Information and Travel Tips for Hanoi

Hanoi, Vietnam's bustling capital, is a city that blends history, culture, and modern life. While exploring this vibrant destination, it's essential to be prepared and informed. Here are some practical tips to help you stay safe, navigate the city, and make the most of your visit.

Health and Safety Tips: Staying Safe and Healthy in Hanoi

Hanoi is generally a safe city for travelers, but like any busy urban center, it's important to exercise caution, especially in crowded areas. Here are some key health and safety tips:

1. Stay Hydrated: The tropical climate in Hanoi can be hot and humid, especially in the summer months. Always carry a bottle of water with you and drink regularly to stay hydrated.

2. Avoid Tap Water: It's recommended not to drink tap water in Hanoi. Stick to bottled water, which is widely available. Make sure the bottle is sealed before purchasing.

3. Food and Hygiene: Hanoi's street food is one of the city's highlights, but always eat at busy food stalls or those recommended by locals to ensure freshness. If you have a sensitive stomach, avoid raw salads and opt for well-cooked meals.

4. Vaccinations: It's a good idea to ensure you're up-to-date on vaccinations before visiting Vietnam, especially for diseases like Hepatitis A, Hepatitis B, and Typhoid. Consult with your healthcare provider before traveling.

5. Traffic Safety: Hanoi's traffic can be overwhelming. Be cautious when crossing streets, as the constant flow of motorbikes can be chaotic. Use pedestrian crossings and follow local advice on how to safely navigate through traffic.

Currency and Payment: The Vietnamese Dong, ATMs, and Credit Cards

The official currency of Vietnam is the Vietnamese Dong (VND). While major tourist areas may accept US dollars, it's best to carry local currency for most transactions. Here's what you need to know about money in Hanoi:

1. ATMs: ATMs are widely available throughout Hanoi, especially in the Old Quarter and near popular tourist sites. Most ATMs dispense

Vietnamese Dong, but some may charge a fee for withdrawals.

2. Currency Exchange: You can exchange currency at banks or authorized exchange centers. Avoid exchanging money with street vendors, as the rates are usually unfavorable.

3. Credit Cards: Credit cards are accepted in many hotels, restaurants, and stores, especially in tourist areas. However, smaller shops, markets, and street vendors typically deal in cash only. It's always a good idea to carry a mix of cash and cards.

Language Tips: Basic Vietnamese Phrases and Communication Advice

Vietnamese is the official language, but English is widely understood in tourist areas, especially among younger generations. However, learning a few basic Vietnamese phrases can help you navigate the city with ease:

1. Hello: "Xin chào" (pronounced sin chow)
2. Thank you: "Cảm ơn" (pronounced gahm un)
3. How much?: "Bao nhiêu?" (pronounced bao nyew)
4. Yes: "Vâng" (pronounced vuhng)
5. No: "Không" (pronounced kohng)

Although many locals can communicate in basic English, particularly in the Old Quarter and near popular tourist attractions, knowing these simple phrases will be appreciated and make your interactions smoother. For more complicated discussions, it's advisable to use a translation app or seek assistance from someone fluent in both languages.

Getting Around Hanoi: Public Transport, Motorbikes, and Walking Tours

Hanoi offers a variety of transportation options, ranging from public transit to more adventurous modes of travel:

1. Public Transport: Hanoi's public transport system is relatively limited, but there are buses that connect most parts of the city. A newer addition is the Hanoi Metro, which provides a convenient way to travel between districts. However, it's still expanding, so buses remain a popular choice.

2. Motorbikes: Motorbikes are the most common form of transportation in Hanoi. You can hire a motorbike taxi (known as xe om) or rent a bike for yourself if you feel comfortable navigating the traffic. Alternatively, you can use ride-hailing apps

like Grab or Gojek, which offer motorbike or car rides.

3. Walking Tours: The best way to explore the heart of Hanoi, especially the Old Quarter, is on foot. Many of the city's attractions are within walking distance of each other, and strolling through the streets allows you to fully immerse yourself in the local atmosphere.

4. Cyclo: For a traditional experience, consider taking a cylo (rickshaw). This relaxing, slow-paced ride is perfect for seeing the sights at a leisurely pace.

Sustainable Travel in Hanoi: Eco-friendly Tips and Responsible Tourism Practices

As a growing tourism destination, Hanoi is increasingly embracing sustainability and eco-friendly practices. Here are some ways you can be a responsible traveler:

1. Respect the Environment: Avoid littering and dispose of your waste properly. Carry a reusable water bottle to reduce plastic waste, and choose eco-friendly products when possible.

2. Support Local Businesses: Shop at local markets, dine at family-run restaurants, and stay at eco-lodges or hotels that practice sustainable tourism. Supporting small local businesses helps boost the economy and preserves Hanoi's cultural heritage.

3. Respect Local Customs and Traditions: Be mindful of local customs, especially when visiting temples or historic sites. Dress modestly when entering places of worship and always ask for permission before taking photos of locals, particularly in rural areas.

4. Reduce Carbon Footprint: Opt for walking or cycling tours rather than using taxis for short distances. Hanoi is a pedestrian-friendly city, and by exploring on foot or by bike, you contribute to reducing pollution and conserving energy.

5. Conserve Water and Energy: At your accommodation, remember to turn off lights and air conditioning when not in use and minimize water consumption.

By following these eco-friendly tips and being mindful of the local culture, you can help preserve Hanoi's unique charm while enjoying a sustainable and responsible travel experience.

Conclusion

Hanoi is a city of contrasts, where traditional culture meets modernity. By staying informed about health and safety, understanding local customs, and using transportation responsibly, you can enjoy a rewarding and hassle-free visit. Embrace sustainable travel practices, and you'll not only contribute to the conservation of the city's heritage but also experience Hanoi in a more authentic and meaningful way.

Made in United States
Orlando, FL
09 December 2024

55308306R00055